NRI'S CHEAT SHEET

9 Essential Things Every NRI Must Do During Their Next Visit to India

Neeraj Arora

Alpha Publishers, India

Mr. Radha Krishan Arora

To my late father, who showed me the power of hard work and determination. Your lessons have shaped my character and this book. Your legacy lives on through these pages.

This book is dedicated to my late father, Mr. Radha Krishan Arora.

I learned banking from my maternal late grandfather, Krishan Lal Jawa, and my mother, Sudesh Arora - both retired from the largest bank in India, the State Bank of India.

But it was my father who ignited my passion for investing at the age of 16. He didn't just introduce me to the world of investments; he walked me through my first deadly encounter with the market.

He guided me through the highs and lows of the stock market and gave me support during a volatile market. He is the one who first showed me the secret to making a spectacular return on investment.

Not all of his stock investments proved to be profitable, as is typical with stock investing. But he never lost faith in investing, continued to learn and invest for the long term, and built an outstanding portfolio. At the age of 77, he was actively managing a robust stock portfolio that included blue-chip securities he had held for three decades. He even bought several equities for long-term investing just a few days before he left us.

Investments were our favorite topic to discuss, and we would regularly talk about them for hours over the weekend. I dearly miss those conversations, filled with wisdom and shared dreams.

Contents

Introduction

Why Planning Ahead is a Key
for NRIs Visiting India

Hey there! Congratulations on getting this book!

For every NRI going to India for a visit, they get all nostalgic and want to do a bunch of stuff? Well, here's a list of things that they usually want to do:

- Eat lots of yummy food

- Hang out with friends

- Go to places they remember from their childhood

- Celebrate festivals

- Visit siblings and cousins

- Help their parents/in-laws with banking and money stuff

- Take care of their parents' and in-laws' health

- Run errands for their parents and in-laws

- Visit their grandparents and their spouse's grandparents

- Meet lots of family and friends and eat at their houses

- Try out Ayurveda and relaxation stuff

- Go on a spiritual trip

There is hardly enough time to do these activities on a trip to India. It is challenging to find time for the activities they truly desire, as well as banking and administrative tasks. It could be to change the status of an account opened during studies or the change in resident status for investments.

But here's the thing: **neglecting these tasks now could have serious consequences down the road**. It could lead to a notice, penalty, or both from FEMA and/or Income Tax departments.

NRIs usually know that these things are important, so they try to do them when they come to India. But it's really hard to do everything and still have enough time for other activities. Sometimes, it feels like they're not even on vacation because they have so much to do!

So, if you're an NRI, how do you take care of important stuff while you're in India? How can you have a real vacation and not just a **"personal leave with work"**?

The solution? Get organized and make a plan! You should make a list of the most important things you need to do while you're in India. The items mentioned in this book are based on research and conversations with lots of people who have visited India before. Some tasks that required you to be in India, can now be done from your country of residence, so these items are not included in the main To-Do list. Make sure you prioritize the most important tasks and set aside time to get them done. This will help you stay on track and not have to sacrifice other important parts of your life.

Happy Holidays in India!

As a postgraduate in finance with a law degree in taxation from India, having worked over 20 years in the banking and finance industry, I have a fair amount of experience in this area. I've worked in different countries, like India, Singapore, France, and Switzerland. I've met a lot of people who live outside of India, including many of my own family members who live across five continents and in places like Europe, the United States, Japan, Canada, and Australia. When we talk, banking and administrative tasks in India are a common topic of worry and somehow do come into the discussion.

I wrote this book to help NRIs who live outside of India. It's all about focusing on the most important things during your next trip so that you can save time and spend more quality time with your loved ones.

Bonus spoiler: If you have kids who you would like to get more engaged and connected with India, there are activities and tips in this book that will also help your kids feel more connected with India. The information contained in this book has already helped a lot of people save time in **two primary ways**:

First, they were able to take care of some actions from their country of residence instead of waiting until their next India visit. This made their to-do list shorter.

Second, they had a prioritized list of things to do months before their trip. Some people even planned their trip around this list and were able to complete everything in a short amount of time.

The book is short and easy to read, and it has spaces for you to write down actions you need to take. Research shows that writing down actions after reading makes it more likely that you'll actually take them.

So, if you're an NRI (Non-Resident Indian) or a PIO (Person of Indian Origin) or an OCI Cardholder (Overseas Citizenship of India), I encourage you to read this book right away so you can get the most out of your next India visit.

Don't wait!!!

Important

Before you start reading

Although NRI, PIO, and OCI cardholders are different as per Indian law, there are similarities in terms of taxation and investment regulations.

For simplicity, only the term NRI has been used throughout the book. It can be interpreted to apply to NRI, PIO, and OCI cardholders.

* * *

Non Resident Indian (NRI): An Indian citizen who is ordinarily residing outside India and holds an Indian Passport.

Person of Indian Origin (PIO): A person who or whose any of ancestors was an Indian national and who is presently holding another country's citizenship/ nationality i.e. he/ she is holding foreign passport.

Overseas Citizen of India (OCI) Cardholder: A person registered as Overseas Citizen of India (OCI) Cardholder under section 7A of the Citizenship Act, 1955.

1. VERIFY / UPDATE PAN CARD

Permanent Account Number (Pan)

Did you know that less than 1% Indians update their PAN after becoming an NRI?

This is probably the most neglected area for NRIs. Verify that address and other details in your, and your spouse's PAN card and if required please ensure that they are updated. Many NRIs still have a PAN card as a resident. Although the address is not visible in your PAN card, it needs to be updated in PAN records in the Income Tax department.

Aadhaar

An NRI is not required to have an Aadhar Card and many NRIs do not have an Aadhar card. In case you, your spouse and your kid(s) have an Aadhar card, verify the details and if required please update them during your next India visit.

Link PAN Card to Aadhaar

In case you have a PAN Card as well as an Aadhar card, Linking your PAN to Aadhar is recommended. Although it's not mandatory for an NRI, it's recommended to avoid unnecessary paperwork and admin work in future.

The good news is that this can be linked online, and you don't have to be in India for this. To verify your PAN card, you can visit the official website of the Income Tax Department or use the NSDL portal. You will need to enter your PAN number and other personal details to complete the verification process.

It is crucial to keep these documents updated and accurate as any discrepancies can lead to complications in financial transactions or availing government schemes. So, take some time out and ensure that your PAN card and Aadhaar card details are up-to-date.

Potential consequences: It's important to keep your PAN and Aadhaar details up-to-date and linked if you have an Aadhaar card. In the event of discrepancies between PAN and Aadhaar card details, you could face some serious problems. Your financial transactions might not go through, your PAN might become inactive, and you could get in trouble with the law. If your PAN becomes inactive, you won't be able to file your taxes or get any refunds. If your PAN is active but has old information, you might end up paying the wrong amount of taxes and getting penalties from the Tax Department.

Case Study: In one of the cases I personally know, Mr. Gaurav (name changed) didn't update his Indian address as he had left the city and stayed in Europe. The Indian Income Tax Department issued a notice demanding to pay some taxes and sent it to his registered address as per his PAN card. Mr. Gaurav never received the demand letter from the Income Tax Department as he had left the country. As he had no income in India, he never filed an indian tax return. He also never updated his address on his PAN card. As the Tax Department never received an explanation or response from Mr. Gaurav, they made the assessment with "No show" and issued a demand letter asking to deposit the initial amount with interest and penalty. The total amount continued to increase due to compound interest. It was three years after Mr. Gaurav came to know about it. It was only possible when Mr. Gaurav wanted to sell his apartment. Mr. Gaurav spent significant money, time, and efforts to settle this case.

All of these could have been avoided by simply updating the PAN card details. Mr. Gaurav also became subject to higher scrutiny in future IT returns, not the attention an NRI would like to have.

To avoid these issues, make sure your information is up-to-date in PAN and Aadhaar and that your PAN Card and Aadhaar are linked.

* * *

Key takeaways

1. _______________________________

2. _______________________________

3. _______________________________

4. _______________________________

5. _______________________________

Actions

1. _______________________________

2. _______________________________

3. _______________________________

4. _______________________________

5. _______________________________

2. CONSOLIDATE AND UPDATE BANK ACCOUNTS WITH NRO STATUS

With the latest trends in online banking, opening a new account online is super easy, convenient, and doesn't take up a lot of time. Some people in India (Residents and Non-residents alike) have a lot of bank accounts, but this can be a lot of work to keep track of. It's best to have just two or three. And in the case of non-resident Indians, it's better to go with a big private bank because they usually have better services for you.

As per law, responsibilities lie with you to inform your

bank or financial intermediary about your residential status, including any change in residential status. In addition to your savings bank account, you also need to update the resident status as non-resident for any other type of Bank account including fixed deposits, loan accounts, and bank locker, etc. It's important to keep your information up-to-date across all types of accounts so everything runs smoothly.

Consolidate and update all your savings bank accounts with NRO Status

It is normally a good idea to consolidate your Indian bank accounts to the extent possible and have a relationship with a couple of banks. This will make it easier to take care of them from another country, and you won't have to do as much paperwork. While consolidating, keep in mind the online banking facilities and support provided by banks from abroad. Not all Indian banks are suitable for NRI customers, as some do not have the necessary infrastructure and/or poor paper-based processes that might require NRIs to visit a branch more frequently, which is a challenge in the case of an NRI. In my personal experience, big private banks in India are providing better services to NRIs as compared to government banks. But government banks are also catching up fast.

Non-Resident External (NRE) Account

Open an NRE account or Non-Resident External (NRE) account, in case you do not have one. Most people are familiar with NRE accounts. In short, an NRE account is used to deposit funds generated from foreign countries back to India. Funds in your NRE Savings account are fully repatriable.

Fixed Deposits

If you have a Fixed Deposit (FD) linked to your bank account, the status should update to NRO automatically. But it's always a good idea to double-check with your bank just in case. Some banks have different rules, or you might have more than one customer ID with the bank. If that's the case, you might need to give them more documents. So, it's important to ask your bank if they need anything else.

Watch out- If you have an independent Fixed Deposit, which is not linked to your savings account, the process might be different and/or tricky. It is very important to ask your bank if they need anything else. It is important to keep a close eye on FDs not linked to accounts.

Demat Accounts

If you have some stocks in your Demat account, you need to make sure it's updated to NRO status too. Similar to interest on a savings account, the dividend on equity shares in an NRO demat account attracts tax deduction at the source (TDS).

As an NRI, you earn income outside India, and if you want to invest this money (earned outside) in stocks in India, you should open an NRE Demat account. You can do this from abroad, but it's easier if you do it in person when you visit India.

Note: A demat account is an Indian term for a dematerialized account that holds financial securities digitally and to trade shares in the stock market.

Demat accounts also have PINS (Portfolio Investment Scheme) and Non-PINS concept, which is different from the repatriable (NRE) and non-repatriable (NRO) concept. To avoid further complications on this topic, you can assume that PINS accounts are required to purchase shares in India. You can have only one PINS account in India. Once a PINS account is opened with a bank, it is difficult and time-consuming to move your PINS account to another bank. Additionally, it can incur significant cost.

You should open a demat account only if you are an advanced investor and have the time, professional skills, and willingness to invest in the stock market after properly analyzing stocks.

Mutual Funds /ETFs are normally a better investment vehicle as they are simple, cost-effective, and easy to manage from abroad.

> **Tip:** If you're married and have a good relationship with your spouse, it's better to open a joint account with your spouse so you can keep using it together, and it's an advantage in case one of you is not available to access the account.

Update Home Loan Bank status

If you have a home loan, it's important to tell your bank about changes in your resident status to a non-resident. That way, they can help you out and make sure everything is still okay. You should also let the builder know about any changes. It's always better to keep everyone in the loop!

Bank Locker

If you don't need it a locker, surrender it! There are some new rules that are making it tough for NRIs to manage the locker. If you need to keep the locker, you need to inform your bank about your NRI status as well.

* * *

Key takeaways

1. ______________________________

2. ______________________________

3. ______________________________

4. ______________________________

5. ______________________________

Actions

1. ______________________________

2. ______________________________

3. ______________________________

4. ______________________________

5. ______________________________

3. SUBMIT NEW KYC DETAILS AND UPDATE FATCA STATUS FOR MUTUAL FUND INVESTMENTS

This is also one area that is not promptly addressed by NRIs. This can be avoided by submitting a few documents in case investors have been informed. Till a few years ago, this was not an issue, but in recent years, the mutual fund industry has seen significant changes in regulations and technological advancement. There are strict regulations and rules about how much money they can receive from NRIs.

Also, if you have something called an SIP (Systematic Investment Plan), some mutual fund companies won't let you continue it if you live in certain countries. It's a good idea to check with the mutual fund company to see if you can invest from your country of residence. If you don't, you might run into some issues later. So, be sure to do your research before investing or talk to a Mutual Fund Distributor who can help you take the necessary steps.

Key takeaways

1. _______________________________

2. _______________________________

3. _______________________________

4. _______________________________

5. _______________________________

Actions

1. _______________________________

2. _______________________________

3. _______________________________

4. _______________________________

5. _______________________________

4. OPEN A JOINT ACCOUNT WITH YOUR PARENT OR GRANDPARENT

Did you know that as an NRI, you can now open a joint bank account with your parents in India?

NRIs can now open a joint account with a close relative who is a resident of India - for instance their parents, siblings, spouse, children, grandparents, grandchildren, etc.

The joint account type will be "**Former or Survivor**". Your close resident relative (e.g., mother) will be the main account holder, while you'll be the secondary one. That means your mother (Former) can use the account while she is alive, but after she passes away, the account will be in your name (Survivor) and will also be converted into an NRO account. There are some regulations around investment in this account. Please check with your bank and Indian Tax Advisor for restrictions.

This is not something known to people and perhaps one of the most NRI-friendly steps taken by the RBI (Reserve Bank of India).

❋ ❋ ❋

Key takeaways

1. _______________________________

2. _______________________________

3. _______________________________

4. _______________________________

5. _______________________________

Actions

1. _______________________________

2. _______________________________

3. _______________________________

4. _______________________________

5. _______________________________

5. ACQUIRE AN INDIAN PHONE NUMBER

This is something I have avoided in the past for a long time. I used to use my parents' extra prepaid phone number, but one time my dad forgot to charge it, and the SIM became inactive. I had to face many problems, and I had to spend a long time updating my phone number in all my banks and other records. Since then, I have maintained my personal Indian number.

Now, the Indian government, banks, and regulators are making a new rule that says each person should have their own phone number. If you use the same number as your family members, your bank will ask you to update it. This rule is also being applied to email.

Having your own phone number has two additional benefits:

1) You don't have to give your friends and family a new number every time you visit.

2) You can manage your bank accounts and other important things from another country if you have an Indian phone number.

* * *

Key takeaways

1. ________________________________

2. ________________________________

3. ________________________________

4. ________________________________

5. ________________________________

Actions

1. ________________________________

2. ________________________________

3. ________________________________

4. ________________________________

5. ________________________________

6. BUY TERM INSURANCE

Life is unpredictable, and 3D (Death, Disease, and Disability) can affect your financial stability and goals. Protect your family so that they continue to pursue their dreams. Most people are either under-insured or over-insured. Many NRIs have coverage in their country of residence through their job. This is good only until you have a job. If you plan to do business or return to India, this insurance will not be valid.

Many NRIs are unaware that term insurance purchased in India is valid worldwide. In most cases, the cost of purchasing term insurance in India is significantly lower than purchasing it in their home country. Because NRI insurance coverage is typically higher, a medical examination in India is required.

So, if you intend to buy, you can save a significant amount of time if you analyze and finalize the best plan for you before traveling to India. When you arrive in India, the execution and medical procedures can begin. This is one of the areas where your financial advisor can assist you. It is even better if you can find someone who is familiar with your country of residence.

Key takeaways

1. ____________________________________

2. ____________________________________

3. ____________________________________

4. ____________________________________

5. ____________________________________

Actions

1. ____________________________________

2. ____________________________________

3. ____________________________________

4. ____________________________________

5. ____________________________________

7. HEALTH CHECK-UP & UPDATE HEALTH RECORDS

A vital item to tackle on your next India visit is getting a complete physical and updating your medical documents.

During your India visit, also encourage your parents and family members to undergo health checkups and update their medical records. This proactive approach will help you and your family identify any potential health issues early on and enable timely medical intervention, if needed.

In one scenario, my friend's father required a long recovery period after major stomach surgery and required testing on a weekly basis. My friend flew to India, but he could only go for two weeks. As my friend has soft copies of his father's medical records, he collaborated with his brother and sister, who were also living abroad, and monitored progress from abroad. His fulfillment and contentment, as he told me about it, were indescribable.

*　*　*

Key takeaways

1. _______________________________

2. _______________________________

3. _______________________________

4. _______________________________

5. _______________________________

Actions

1. _______________________________

2. _______________________________

3. _______________________________

4. _______________________________

5. _______________________________

8. CONSULT PROFESSIONALS (CHARTERED ACCOUNTANTS, LAWYERS ETC.)

Most NRIs will require the services of a chartered accountant or a lawyer at some point in their lives. When you are in India, you should visit the CA or lawyer and evaluate his/her capabilities by visiting his or her office.

Typically, NRIs seek the services of a CA or a lawyer after their situation has deteriorated. NRIs ask a friend or relative for the name of a CA or lawyer and normally do not have enough time to evaluate the professional due to time constraints. It is highly recommended that you visit the CA and the lawyer during your India visit and seek advance guidance about future financial transactions so that you can make an informed and law-abiding decision.

Finding a suitable lawyer is also advantageous if you own property or have a complicated family situation. The lawyer can assist you in drafting the **power of attorney (PoA)** required to sell your property, as well as drafting and registering a **will** for you or your parents.

A CA or lawyer in India can provide you with information about Indian laws, but you must be familiar with the laws of your home country. Something that is not taxable in India may be taxed differently in another country. A gift to a brother, for example, is not taxable in India, but it is mostly taxable (with some limits and exemptions) in Switzerland and varies depending on the canton or state in which you live. The same is true in the United States, where gifts are taxable after a certain amount.

It is typically difficult to find a lawyer or CA, who is experienced and knowledgeable about taxation rules in India and as well as in your country of residence.

* * *

Key takeaways

1. _______________________________

2. _______________________________

3. _______________________________

4. _______________________________

5. _______________________________

Actions

1. _______________________________

2. _______________________________

3. _______________________________

4. _______________________________

5. _______________________________

9. MANAGE PROPERTY ACCOUNTS AND AGENTS/ CONTRACTOR

Home holds sentimental value for most Indians, making it an area that requires significant time commitment and oversight. Here are some important things to take care of during your next visit to India.

Take Inventory Of House Related Accounts

If you have properties, take inventory of your property-related accounts (house tax, maintenance, home loan, etc.) and register for online services if not already done.

Meet the builder and contractor and inform them about change in your status

Meet with builders and contractors for ongoing home construction to assess the current construction progress and plan upcoming milestones. Check to see if you need to give your parents or a family member a power of attorney to take possession from the builder if you are not going to be present for possession.

Plan your sale and meet a property agent or dealer

If you intend to sell your property, you should consult with a real estate dealer or agent. It is very common for NRIs to receive an overpriced value when purchasing a property and an underpriced value when selling a property. Before disclosing your NRI status, you should inquire about the price with the property dealer or agent. This will assist you in determining your property's fair market value. This will not help you if you try to sell after a few months, but at least you had a fair value to compare with in future.

Key takeaways

1. _______________________________

2. _______________________________

3. _______________________________

4. _______________________________

5. _______________________________

Actions

1. _______________________________

2. _______________________________

3. _______________________________

4. _______________________________

5. _______________________________

BONUS 1: SPEND QUALITY TIME WITH PARENTS AND FRIENDS

Plan A Vacation During Vacation

This is the only non-financial tip in this book. For NRIs, the happiness of reuniting with their families and friends is unparalleled. NRIs enjoy spending time with their parents and siblings, as well as with their friends and relatives. This is occasionally interrupted by the banking and investment administrative activities mentioned above. While all of the activities listed above are vital, it is equally crucial to spend undisturbed time with your parents and family in India.

Plan a short holiday trip in advance

Many NRIs have shared that a short holiday trip of 3-5 days with parents and family has created the most pleasant memories for them. For planning purposes, a trip after a couple of days of immediate landing is optimal. It is recommended to book this trip before you land in India to make it happen. I have tried to go on a trip every single time I visit India. Many of my memorable experiences with my parents and in-laws were also created during these short trips.

Key takeaways

1. ____

2. ____

3. ____

4. ____

5. ____

Actions

1. ____

2. ____

3. ____

4. ____

5. ____

BONUS 2: IMPORTANT ITEMS YOU CAN DO FROM ABROAD

Many things that used to require a trip to India are now feasible from your country of residence, thanks to technological improvements and improved governance. For example, you may open an NRE and NRO account in your name, jointly with your spouse, or in the name of your minor children from abroad.

The activities listed below are significant for NRIs, although they do not need a trip to India. You can do it from your country of residence.

1. Obtain and update the PAN card

2. Link Aadhaar with PAN

3. Open a bank account in the name of you, your spouse, or your child

4. Open Demat account in the name of you, your spouse, or your child

5. File your Income Tax Return as an NRI

6. Fill out forms from banks and financial institutions before traveling to India

7. Complete the gift deed formalities if you received money as a gift from your parents or/and in-laws

8. Retirement planning: Even if you are undecided about where to retire

❋ ❋ ❋

Key takeaways

1. ______________________________

2. ______________________________

3. ______________________________

4. ______________________________

5. ______________________________

Actions

1. ______________________________

2. ______________________________

3. ______________________________

4. ______________________________

5. ______________________________

CONCLUSION

Make the Most of Your Visit to India by Planning Ahead and Experiencing All That This Incredible Country Has to Offer

This book contains a list of items that can serve as a guide for NRIs during their journey to India. These items are meant to help them achieve their goals. However, not all items may be relevant to every individual, so it is important to determine relevant and meaningful actions for you.

The book emphasizes the importance of preparing ahead of time for certain items, as they may require lead time. This means that you should start planning and taking action on these items well in advance to ensure they are addressed during your trip.

To determine crucial items for you, it would be helpful to review the specific list mentioned in the book. From there, you can prioritize the items based on your personal goals and needs. It is also important to consider the lead time for items, as this will impact when you need to begin addressing them.

The key takeaway is to start planning and taking action on the items that are relevant to you right now. This could involve researching and making arrangements for accommodations, transportation, visa requirements, or any other specific goals you have for your trip to India.

By beginning the preparation process early, you can ensure a smoother and more organized journey to India. As said, the key thing is that you begin **RIGHT NOW**.

Review the notes and actions you have taken after each chapter, prepare an action list, and prioritize them as per your personalized situation. If in doubt, contact your financial advisor.

On the next two pages, you may print a checklist and a blank To-Do list. If you prefer an Excel or PDF version, go to the www.nrifs.com resources area and download the blank checklist in various file formats.

✻ ✻ ✻

FREE RESOURCES & DOWNLOADABLE

Checklist

#	Item	Priority	Progress/Comments
	Essential Things To Do During Next Visit to India		
1	Verify/Update PAN Card		
2	Consolidate and Update Bank Accounts with NRO Status		
3	Submit new KYC details and update FATCA status for Mutual Fund Investments		
4	Open a Joint account with your parent or grandparent		
5	Acquire an Indian Phone number		
6	Buy Term Insurance		
7	Health Check-up & Update Health Records		
8	Consult professionals (Chartered Accountants, Lawyers etc.)		
9	Manage Property Accounts and Agents/Contractor		
10	Bonus 1: Spend quality time with Parents and friends		
11	Bonus 2: Important items you can do from abroad		
12			
13			
14			

Download - Checklist

Method 1:

Go to *www.nrifs.com* --> Resources --> Books

Method 2: Scan the QR code below

Blank To Do List

TO-DO LIST

High Priority

#	Action	Status	Progress/Comments
1			
2			
3			
4			
5			
6			

Medium Priority

#	Action	Status	Progress/Comments
1			
2			
3			
4			
5			
6			

Low Priority

#	Action	Status	Progress/Comments
1			
2			
3			
4			
5			
6			

Other tasks/Actions

#	Action	Status	Progress/Comments
1			
2			
3			
4			
5			
6			

Download - Blank To Do List

Method 1:

Go to *www.nrifs.com* --> Resources --> Books

Method 2: Scan the QR code below

Acknowledgments

Writing a book was harder than I thought, yet more rewarding than I could have ever imagined. None of this would have been possible without

my wife, **Mishi.** She has always been there for me and has supported me through all my life adventures.

my daughter, **Nishka,** who is currently studying economics and law. I have taught her many things and also learned a lot from her.

I want to thank

my brothers (Dheeraj Kumar Arora and Hemant Arora) and sisters-in-laws (Preeti Arora and Shruti Bali) for trusting me and showering me with an abundance of love and respect.

my sister-in-law (Prachi Arora) and brother-in-law (Rohit Arora) for their love, respect, and trust in me. Their presence adds depth and color to my life.

My mother, Sudesh Arora, who has always shown me unconditional love.

My mother-in-law, Manisha Agarwal, who has supported me in writing this book.

My Nibling - nieces (Anshika, Ishika) & nephews (Aarav, Hayden, and Shaun).

My extended family members.

Furthermore, I am grateful for my professors and mentors in life: Andreas Gschmeidler, my uncle Ashok Arora, K. N. Arora (RIP), Rajesh Malhotra, S. C. Gupta (RIP), and Sanjay Joshi.

Finally, to all those who have been a part of my journey of getting here:

Andreas Schneider, Anil Shukla, Davinder Singh, Dheeraj Tyagi, Gwen Lim, Hugo Chestier, Lawrence Yeo, Mani Ratnasamy, Manish Prajapati, Manoj Kumar, Matthew Antkowiak, Neha Prajapati, Nirupam Chaturvedi (RIP), Nitesh Ghandhi, Rajeev

Arora, Rajender Reddy, Sameer Kumar, Sanjeev Gupta, Sanjeev Kumar, Sherwin Siregar, Tanushi Tayal (credit: cover design, and editing), Tong Teck Lim, Vivek Arora, Vivek Khurana, Winnie Quek, and Ying Ying Wu.

To everyone mentioned above, as well as those who may not be named but have played a part in making this book, **thank you from the bottom of my heart**. Your contributions are deeply appreciated and will forever be acknowledged within these pages.

About The Author

 Neeraj Arora is a finance professional with a Bachelor of Law (Taxation) and a Post Graduate Diploma in Finance, with 20+ years of experience in the banking and Finance industries across India, Singapore, France, and Switzerland. He has been helping people manage their finances since 2000.

Half of his extended family members live outside India and across all continents—Europe, the United States, Japan, Canada, and Australia—and one of their common topics is pending business in India.

His hobbies include running, listening to music, and playing badminton. He has completed over 40 Half marathons as well as a full marathon in Zurich in 2018.

He has volunteered for a variety of nonprofit professional and social organizations, including PMI Switzerland, ASHA Zurich, the Anouk Foundation, and several Indian associations. He was elected two years in a row and served on the PMI Switzerland chapter's Board of Directors.

In his corporate career, he has written numerous articles and contributed to numerous magazines. His opinions have appeared in international magazines, including Global PMI publications.

You can connect with Author at

LinkedIn: LinkedIn.com/in/neerajaroraswiss

Facebook: facebook.com/neeraj.swiss

Instagram: instagram.com/neeraj.swiss

About NRI Financial Services

NRI Financial Services (NRIFS) is an initiative by Neeraj Arora to assist NRIs, PIOs, and OCI cardholders worldwide in financially securing their future in investment, income tax, or insurance matters. NRIFS aims to help NRIs manage all their financial matters with ease.

The NRIFS team accelerates financial freedom for NRIs, by helping them take advantage of the Indian growth trajectory and maximize returns. NRIFS values relationships, thus encouraging you to live your dream and helping you create stronger bonds with Indian ties.

NRIFS has a presence in India and Switzerland and is affiliated with 25+ financial houses and corporations, such as HDFC, ICICI, Aditya Birla, Kotak, Tata, Invesco, PGIM, Mirae, SBI, and numerous others.

Team NRIFS follows AMFI, SEBI, and IRDA regulations, and is also registered with AMFI and IRDA.

If you wish to know more and to be a part of the NRIFS family, feel free to visit www.nrifs.com or connect on Social Media

LinkedIn   LinkedIn.com/company/NRIFS

Facebook   facebook.com/NRIFinServ

Instagram   instagram.com/NRIFinServ

Occasionally, the NRIFS team provides a **complimentary 30-minute consultation** to NRIs concerning financial and tax-related issues. Visit nrifs.com to find out if this offer is going on. You might be lucky.

You can also join **the weekly newsletter** at nrifs.com. The newsletter provides the latest updates, financial insights, and exclusive content tailored for NRIs. Subscribe today to receive valuable information and stay informed about opportunities and resources for NRIs around the world.

* * *

AMFI - Association of Mutual Funds in India

SEBI - Securities and Exchange Board of India

IRDA - Insurance Regulatory & Development Authority

The Journey Continues

Scan the QR code to **buy this book** and/or **download the free resources** mentioned in this book

An investment in knowledge pays the best interest - Benjamin Franklin